Something Sweet

Something Sweet

TEXT AND RECIPES
BY JACK BISHOP

Illustrated by MATTHEW WAWIORKA
Designed by LYNETTE CORTEZ
Produced by MILLER AND O'SHEA, INC.

SIMON & SCHUSTER
New York London Toronto Sydney Tokyo Singapore

Simon & Schuster
Rockefeller Center
1230 Avenue of the Americas
New York, NY 10020

DESIGNED BY LYNETTE CORTEZ

Manufactured in the United States of America
1 3 5 7 9 10 8 6 4 2

ISBN 0-684-80187-6

To my grandmother,

Dorothy Bishop, baker of my favorite

childhood sweets

Contents

Introduction

A SWEET *for* EVERY CRAVING

Whether it's called a craving, desire, appetite, urge, longing, yen, or yearning, I know the signals.

It's my body's way of telling my head it wants something to eat—now. Sometimes when the craving hits, nothing will satisfy me more than something sweet.

I'm not a big fan of packaged desserts. But when I have a craving, I don't want to spend hours in the kitchen. Too much effort and I'll be too tired to enjoy the fruits of my labor.

This collection of sweets was born out of my passion for fast snacks. All the recipes in this book can be made in less than one hour, most in much less time. I have picked my favorite cookies, puddings, ice cream sundaes, fruit crisps, and brownies and made them easier. Gone are all those tedious steps and pointless ingredients. What's left are desserts that are long on flavor but short on work.

The recipes are organized into five chapters, each addressing a particular type of craving. I love the aroma of just-baked cookies filling the house. There's nothing like noshing on something warm and buttery spiked by chips, nuts, and/or spices. If this is what you're craving, see "Hot from the Oven" for gingerbread, blondies, and other oven-baked treats.

At other times, I want to curl up on the couch with comfort food from my childhood—pudding, tapioca, or ice cream. These smooth, soothing desserts are easy to make and fun to eat. Look for these recipes in the section "Comfort on a Spoon."

Fresh fruit is a staple in my home. Of course, I often pick up a ripe summer peach or winter banana to satisfy a craving. At other times, something more substantial is needed to quell my hunger. Whether it's a perfectly baked apple or a simple (and delicious) plum shortcake, recipes that rely on nature's bounty can be found in "Fruit Favorites."

There are times when only chocolate will do. Whether it's rich, dark pudding or extra-fudgy brownies, I just know I have to have chocolate, and fast. "Chocolate Passions" offers the best quick fixes—like chocolate waffles and easy chocolate souffles—when the urge for chocolate borders on obsession.

Finally, there are times when I crave sweets but want to maintain my healthy eating regimen. There's no need to go into withdrawal. "Healthy Indulgences" enables you to give in to your craving sensibly. The recipes here are either low-fat or non-fat, and skimp on calories but not flavor.

A final note about using this book. Each recipe is keyed for preparation time. Many recipes are simple and fast to make. Others take a little longer to prepare (most of the time is spent waiting for items to bake and/or cool) but are just as easy to execute. If you just can't wait, choose a recipe that can be completed in minutes. If you can hold out for 30 minutes or more, then you'll find other sweets to savor. Just refer to the time note in each recipe. There are plenty of delicious options to satisfy every kind of craving for something sweet.

A SWEET LOVER'S PANTRY

It's a good idea to keep
a number of basic staples on hand;
you never know when a craving will strike. Here's
a list of essential ingredients along with some general notes on
their use in desserts.

BAKING POWDER & BAKING SODA: At least one
and sometimes both of these rising agents is used in baked
goods. Baking powder contains baking soda and an activating
acid called cream of tartar. In a pinch, 1/3 teaspoon baking soda
plus 2/3 teaspoon cream of tartar can be used for each teaspoon
of baking powder. There is no substitute for baking soda.

BUTTER: I prefer the flavor of butter in desserts and do not
recommend the use of margarine. In addition to taste consider-
ations, recent studies have shown that the benefit of using margarine may have been previously overestimated. All my recipes
call for sweet (unsalted) butter. I prefer its cleaner flavor and like
to add salt as I deem necessary.

CHOCOLATE: There are several kinds of chocolate used in
this book. Unsweetened baking chocolate has a pure chocolate

flavor with no added sugar. There are no substitutes for this kind of chocolate. Although semisweet chocolate usually contains a bit more sugar than bittersweet, the two can be used interchangeably.

COCOA: Unsweetened cocoa contains a fraction of the fat found in regular chocolate but still delivers a strong chocolate punch. European-style cocoa, also called Dutch cocoa, is more mellow than American cocoa like Hershey's. I prefer the strength of American cocoa in baked goods and use tamer European cocoa in puddings and sauces. However, the two are interchangeable in all recipes.

EGGS: All recipes call for large eggs. Keep eggs in the refrigerator until ready to use since cold eggs will separate into whites and yolks more easily.

FLOUR: All recipes in this book use all-purpose flour. To measure correctly, dip cup into flour and sweep excess from top with a small spatula or knife. Flour should be even with the lip of the measuring cup.

MILK & CREAM: Recipes were tested with whole milk, although all can be made with low-fat. I don't recommend skim

milk since texture and flavor may suffer. To whip heavy cream, chill it thoroughly and use a bowl and beaters that also have been well chilled. When making sweetened whipped cream, you can preserve the silky texture by using confectioners' sugar instead of granulated.

NUTS: Walnuts, pecans, almonds, macadamias, and pine nuts add crunch and flavor to many sweets. Store nuts in the refrigerator to prevent their natural oils from becoming rancid.

SALT: Many sweet recipes call for small quantities of salt to balance out the sugar and other flavors. Amounts per serving are tiny and salt should not be omitted unless necessary for health reasons.

SPICES: Ground cinnamon, ginger, cloves, and allspice add an enticing flavor and aroma to many cookies, cakes, and other desserts. After several years, ground spices can lose some of their potency and should be replaced.

SUGAR: Granulated white sugar is used in recipes unless otherwise noted. Brown sugar, which has a richer, more intense flavor, is used when a hint of caramel is desired. Light and dark brown sugar can be used interchangeably unless one is specifically called for in a recipe. Confectioners' or powdered sugar is used to sweeten whipped cream and garnish desserts. Simply place a teaspoon or two in a mesh strainer and gently shake over cakes, puddings, or cookies to add an elegant touch.

VANILLA EXTRACT: Always use pure extract—never artificial versions. Vanilla extract complements and intensifies other flavors, especially fruit and chocolate. Vanilla extract will keep indefinitely in the cupboard.

VEGETABLE OIL: Use a neutral-tasting oil like canola in desserts. Reserve strong oils like olive for savory dishes.

TOP TEN
SHORTCUTS

The recipes in this book are all easy to make, but some basic cooking knowledge is required. Here's a list of the most important kitchen tricks I use to speed my work and ensure perfect results.

1 Sifting flour is a messy, time-consuming step that can be eliminated from many recipes, including all those in this book. Instead of sifting, I combine dry ingredients like salt, baking powder, and flour with a metal whisk. A quick stir with a whisk not only removes lumps but adds volume to the flour (a process called aeration) much like sifting.

2 Many recipes call for greasing pans and baking sheets. Use vegetable oil spray unless otherwise instructed. It's fast, covers evenly, and has less saturated fat than butter.

3 The size and material of the pan is extremely important. Some metal pans can react with acids and sugar and should not be used when recipes specify glass or ceramic pans. On the other hand, metal baking pans are usually the best choice in the oven; glass and ceramic can overheat and cause burning around the edges. Note recipes made in larger or smaller pans than called for will not bake properly.

4 Butter will soften on the counter in 30 to 60 minutes, depending on the room temperature of your kitchen. For faster results, place butter in a glass bowl and cover loosely with plastic wrap. Microwave on high for 10 seconds. Check to see if butter has softened enough. If not, continue to microwave butter for 10-second intervals until softened. Larger quantities (such as a whole stick) will most likely require a total of 20 or 30 seconds.

5 Melting chocolate must be done with care. If just chocolate (or chocolate and butter) is set directly over the heat source it can burn. (Chocolate can be melted on the stove if combined with liquid ingredients like milk, which will prevent scorching.) Use a double boiler to slowly melt chocolate. If you don't have a double boiler you can improvise with a metal bowl set over a pot of gently simmering water. Better yet, place chocolate (and butter, if called for) in a glass bowl and microwave on medium for 45 seconds. Stir and continue to microwave at 15-second intervals until completely melted. Stir chocolate until smooth and proceed with recipe.

6 Immediately transfer hot cookies or pans from the oven onto wire cooling racks. This prevents pans from scorching your counter and speeds cooling since air can circulate underneath. Faster cooling means faster snacking.

7 Recipes always call for preheating the oven first. By the time the batter is ready, the oven will be hot.

8 Smaller portions mean less work. For this reason, recipes in this book generally serve just four. Most cookie recipes make two batches that can be baked at the same time. Of course, recipes can be doubled, but expect to double your work as well.

9 Cooking times may be less than recipes suggest. For instance, your oven may run hotter than it should. For this reason, test baked goods several minutes before you think they will be done. You can always close the oven and bake for several more minutes, but once something has burned, it's ruined.

10 This last tip is the most important: Read the recipe all the way through before doing anything. Steps are listed in the order that guarantees quickest results. Knowing what comes next always saves time and effort.

the Oven.

Blondies with Chocolate Peanut Butter Frosting

Makes 12 bars
Time: 55 minutes
(including 20 minutes for cooling)

These frosted blondies--a divine combination of butterscotch, peanut butter, and chocolate--take about 30 minutes to prepare, bake, and glaze. However, allow at least 20 minutes for glaze to set before cutting into individual bars.

Blondies
12 tablespoons (1½ sticks) unsalted butter, softened
⅔ cup firmly packed brown sugar
1 large egg
1½ teaspoons vanilla extract
1⅓ cups flour
½ teaspoon baking powder

Chocolate-Peanut Butter Frosting
¾ cup semisweet chocolate chips
¼ cup creamy peanut butter

1. Preheat oven to 350°. Grease an 8-inch-square baking pan.
2. Cream butter and sugar until light and fluffy. Add egg and vanilla and beat until smooth. Stir in flour and baking powder until just combined.
3. Spread batter (it will be fairly stiff) evenly into prepared pan, using fingers or a spatula. Bake until a toothpick inserted in the center of the pan comes out clean, 18 to 20 minutes. Cool pan on rack for 5 minutes.
4. While blondies are cooling, combine chocolate chips and peanut butter in a small saucepan set over low heat. Stir until chocolate has melted and glaze is smooth.
5. Spread glaze evenly over the top of the blondies. Cool for at least 20 minutes to allow glaze to harden and set before cutting into bars.

Cappuccino Biscotti With Chocolate Chips

Makes 24 large biscotti
Time: 55 minutes

Biscotti, which means "twice cooked" in Italian, must bake longer than most cookies. But there is no need to divide dough into individual portions or stand by the oven and make batch after batch. Just shape dough into long logs and then slice into individual cookies after the first baking. The biscotti are then baked again for five minutes to crisp the edges.

> 2 cups flour
> 1 cup sugar
> ½ teaspoon ground cinnamon
> ½ teaspoon baking powder
> ½ teaspoon baking soda
> ½ teaspoon salt
> 2 tablespoons milk
> ¼ cup prepared espresso or strong coffee, cooled slightly
> 1 large egg yolk

1 teaspoon vanilla extract
⅔ cup whole almonds, chopped coarse
½ cup semisweet chocolate chips

1. Preheat oven to 375°. Grease and flour a large baking sheet.
2. In an electric mixer, blend flour, sugar, cinnamon, baking powder, baking soda, and salt briefly.
3. Stir milk into espresso along with egg yolk and vanilla extract. Mix well and add to dry ingredients. Beat on low setting until dough is smooth, about 1 minute. Fold in nuts and chocolate chips by hand.
4. Turn dough onto a floured surface and divide in half. With hands, shape each half into a flat log measuring about 12 inches long by 2 inches across. Place logs on prepared baking sheet about 3 inches apart.
5. Bake until logs are firm to the touch, about 30 minutes. Remove baking sheet from oven and reduce heat to 325°. Wearing oven mitts, slice logs crosswise on the diagonal into 1-inch-wide biscotti.
6. Lay cookies cut side down on sheet and return to oven. Bake until cookies are crisp, about 5 minutes. Remove cookies from oven and cool slightly on racks.

Caramel Oatmeal Lace Cookies

Makes 24 large, flat cookies
Time: 35 minutes

These candy-like cookies are chewy, crunchy, crisp, and altogether delectable. Best of all, the dough is ready in less than 10 minutes. These cookies will really spread out in the oven and should be made in three batches; the first two can be baked together. Unfortunately, there are no substitutes for the parchment paper in this recipe. Look for this handy kitchen item in the baking aisle at your supermarket or in cookware stores.

> **12 tablespoons (1½ sticks) unsalted butter**
> **1½ cups old-fashioned (not instant) rolled oats**
> **¾ cup sugar**
> **2 tablespoons flour**
> **½ teaspoon salt**
> **1 teaspoon vanilla extract**
> **1 large egg, lightly beaten**

1. Heat oven to 325°. Line two large baking sheets with parchment paper.
2. Melt butter in a large saucepan. Remove from heat and stir in oats, sugar, flour, salt, and vanilla extract. Mix well with a spoon. Stir in egg.
3. Drop batter by the tablespoon onto the parchment-lined baking sheets, leaving at least 2½ inches between cookies.
4. Bake cookies until edges become golden brown, about 13 minutes. Carefully slide parchment from pan to a rack and give cookies 2 to 3 minutes to harden before transferring them directly to the rack. Repeat with remaining batter.

Chewy Three-Spice Molasses Cookies

Makes 18 large, flat cookies
Time: 25 minutes

A touch of molasses gives these large cookies their rich flavor and chewy texture. If you do not have ground cloves on hand, increase the amount of ginger to 3/4 teaspoon.

1 cup flour
½ teaspoon ground ginger
½ teaspoon ground cinnamon
¼ teaspoon ground cloves
¼ teaspoon salt
¼ teaspoon baking soda
6 tablespoons unsalted butter
½ cup sugar
2 tablespoons molasses
1 large egg

1. Preheat oven to 350°. Line two large baking sheets with aluminum foil.
2. Whisk flour, spices, salt, and baking soda together in a small bowl. Melt butter in a small saucepan.
3. Mix melted butter with sugar and molasses in a large bowl. Lightly beat egg with a fork and stir into butter-sugar mixture. Gently stir in dry ingredients. (Batter will be fairly wet.)
4. Drop batter by rounded tablespoons onto foil-lined baking sheets, leaving at least 2 inches between cookies.
5. Bake until cookies firm up and edges begin to darken slightly, 10 to 12 minutes. Remove baking sheets from oven and transfer foil and cookies to racks. Cool for several minutes, then carefully peel cookies off foil.

Chocolate Coconut Macaroons

Makes 24 cookies
Time: 25 minutes

These tender morsels burst with the flavors of coconut and chocolate. For an even more intriguing snack, add 1 teaspoon grated orange zest or 1 tablespoon orange-flavored liqueur such as Grand Marnier.

> 1 ounce unsweetened chocolate
> ⅔ cup sweetened condensed milk
> 3 cups sweetened flaked coconut
> ½ teaspoon vanilla extract
> ⅛ teaspoon salt
> 1 large egg white

1. Preheat oven to 350°. Grease two large baking sheets.
2. Place chocolate and condensed milk in a large saucepan set over low heat. Stir until chocolate has melted. Remove

from heat and stir in coconut, vanilla extract, and salt. Mix well by hand.

3. Beat egg white until stiff but not dry. Fold gently into batter. Drop batter by rounded tablespoons onto the prepared baking sheets. Use fingers to shape batter into rough balls.

4. Bake cookies until bottoms and edges are set, about 10 minutes. (The tops will appear moist and shiny.) Cool macaroons on a rack.

Double Nut Clusters

Makes 18 large cookies
Time: 25 minutes

Homemade almond paste--nothing more than blanched almonds, sugar, and egg whites--is the basis for these pine nut-covered clusters. The dough can be a bit messy to work with but the results are impressive. For a dressier look, sift confectioners' sugar over cookies just after they come out of the oven. Although I prefer the contrast between the two nuts, the dough can be rolled in more slivered almonds if desired.

1⅔ cups blanched, slivered almonds
1⅓ cups sugar
2 large egg whites
1 cup pine nuts
Confectioners' sugar for dusting, optional

1. Preheat oven to 375°. Grease two large baking sheets.
2. Place almonds and sugar in the workbowl of a large food processor and grind until quite fine. Add egg whites and process until mixture is smooth. (Dough will be wet.)

3. Scrape dough into a bowl. Pour pine nuts into a shallow bowl.
4. Take a rounded tablespoon of the batter and shape into a rough ball about the size of a whole walnut. Roll ball in pine nuts just until outside is covered. Place pine nut-covered balls on baking sheets 2 inches apart.
5. Bake until cookies turn light golden brown in color, 13 to 15 minutes. Be careful not to let nuts burn or turn dark brown. Cool cookies on a rack.
6. If desired, lightly dust cookies with confectioners' sugar while they are cooling.

Lemon Poppy Seed Shortbread

Makes 16 small bars
Time: 40 minutes

These thin, buttery bars are a breeze to make. Bake at a low oven temperature to prevent shortbread from browning. Dress up these lemony treats with a light dusting of confectioners' sugar just before serving.

> 8 tablespoons (1 stick) unsalted butter, softened
> ½ cup confectioners' sugar, plus more for dusting, optional
> 1 teaspoon finely grated lemon zest
> 2 teaspoons fresh lemon juice
> ½ teaspoon vanilla extract
> 1 tablespoon poppy seeds
> 1 cup flour
> ¼ teaspoon salt

1. Preheat oven to 300°. Grease an 8-inch-square baking pan.
2. Cream butter and sugar in an electric mixer until light and fluffy. Add remaining ingredients and mix until just combined.
3. Press dough into prepared pan with fingers. Bake until shortbread is pale gold in color, 30 to 35 minutes. Cool pan on a rack for 5 minutes and cut shortbread into bars.
4. If desired, lightly dust with confectioners' sugar just before serving.

Raspberry Turnovers With White Chocolate

Makes 4 turnovers
Time: 50 minutes
(including 10 minutes for cooling)

Frozen puff pastry is one of those rare convenience products that is actually high-quality. Keep some in the freezer to make these jam-filled turnovers. Feel free to substitute any other fruit jam you desire. You can also skip the chocolate topping and decorate with confectioners' sugar instead. Although the total time may seem a bit long, most of it is spent waiting for puff pastry to thaw and then cool when baked.

> 1 sheet (about ½ pound) frozen puff pastry
> ½ cup seedless raspberry jam
> 1 large egg, beaten well
> 2 teaspoons sugar
> 1 ounce white or semisweet chocolate

1. Remove puff pastry from freezer and thaw at room temperature for 20 minutes.

2. Preheat oven to 425°. Lightly mist a large baking sheet with water.

3. When puff pastry has softened, unfold and then roll into a 12-inch square on a lightly floured counter. Cut rolled puff pastry into four 6-inch squares.

4. Place 2 tablespoons jam in the center of each square and brush edges with a little water. Fold over to make a triangle. Use the tines of a fork to crimp edges shut.

5. Transfer turnovers to baking sheet. Brush tops with beaten egg and sprinkle lightly with sugar. Make three or four short slits on the top of each turnover to allow steam to escape.

6. Bake turnovers until puffed and golden, 12 to 14 minutes. While turnovers are in oven, place chocolate in a zipper-lock plastic bag. Place sealed bag in a glass and fill with very hot tap water to melt chocolate.

7. Transfer baking sheet to a rack. Dry outside of chocolate bag and push chocolate to one corner. Snip a tiny piece from the corner to make an improvised pastry bag and squeeze to drizzle chocolate over the turnovers. Cool for 10 minutes (the filling will be very hot unless you wait) and serve warm.

Walnut Coffee Cake with Brown Sugar Topping

Serves 8
Time: 50 minutes
(including 10 minutes for cooling)

This quick cake is perfect for satisfying a morning craving. It's also a good choice for an afternoon coffee or tea break. Pecans may be used instead of walnuts.

Brown Sugar Topping
½ cup firmly packed light brown sugar
½ cup finely chopped walnuts
2 tablespoons flour
1 teaspoon ground cinnamon
2 tablespoons unsalted butter, softened

Coffee Cake
8 tablespoons (1 stick) unsalted butter, softened
1 cup firmly packed light brown sugar

2 large eggs
1½ cups flour
1½ teaspoons baking powder
½ teaspoon salt
½ cup milk

1. Preheat oven to 375°. Grease a 9-inch-square cake pan.
2. Mix topping ingredients with fingers or fork until butter is cut into very small pieces (pea-sized or smaller) and coated with sugar and nuts. Set aside.
3. For cake batter, cream butter and sugar in an electric mixer until light and fluffy. Add eggs and beat until mixture is smooth, 1 to 2 minutes.
4. Whisk flour, baking powder, and salt together in a small bowl. Add dry ingredients to batter, alternating with some of the milk, and mix until batter is smooth. Pour into prepared pan and sprinkle evenly with reserved topping.
5. Bake until toothpick inserted in center of cake comes out clean and edges begin to pull away from the sides of the pan, about 30 minutes. Cool briefly on a rack and serve warm.

Warm Gingerbread with Spiced Whipped Cream

Serves 6 to 8
Time: 55 minutes
(including 10 minutes for cooling)

This moist gingerbread fills the house with the aroma of ginger and cinnamon. While the cake is in the oven, prepare the Spiced Whipped Cream for a special treat.

Gingerbread
6 tablespoons unsalted butter
½ cup sugar
½ cup molasses
1 large egg
2 cups flour
1 teaspoon baking powder
1 teaspoon baking soda
2 teaspoons ground ginger
1 teaspoon ground cinnamon
¼ teaspoon salt
½ cup milk
¾ cup raisins

Spiced Whipped Cream
½ cup chilled heavy cream
1 teaspoon confectioners' sugar
Pinch (or so) ground ginger

1. Preheat oven to 350°. Grease an 8-inch-square baking pan.
2. Melt butter in a small saucepan. Beat melted butter, sugar, and molasses in an electric mixer for about 1 minute. Beat in egg until smooth.
3. Whisk flour, baking powder, baking soda, ginger, cinnamon, and salt together in a medium bowl.
4. Slowly add dry ingredients to batter, alternating with some of the milk. When all the dry ingredients and milk have been incorporated, stir in raisins. Pour batter into prepared pan.
5. Bake until toothpick inserted in center of cake comes out basically clean (a few crumbs are fine), about 30 minutes. Cool briefly on a rack before serving with Spiced Whipped Cream.
6. For spiced whipped cream, beat chilled heavy cream with a standing or hand mixer. When frothy, add confectioners' sugar, and continue beating until cream holds soft peaks. Stir in a dash or two of ground ginger. Cover and refrigerate until ready to serve.

Comfort

Chocolate Chip Ice Cream Sundae with Mint Raspberry Sauce

Makes 4 sundaes
Time: 10 minutes

A smidgen of potent mint extract provides a subtle but surprising counternote to a cold raspberry sauce. I love the combination of chocolate chip ice cream with raspberries and mint. This is one recipe where frozen fruit is just as good (and a lot less expensive) than fresh. Use the defrost setting on a microwave to thaw frozen berries in just two minutes. For a light treat, serve the nonfat raspberry sauce over frozen yogurt.

12 ounces frozen raspberries, thawed, or 1 pint fresh
3 to 4 tablespoons sugar (adjust amount depending on sweetness of berries)
1 tablespoon lemon juice
¼ teaspoon mint extract
1½ pints chocolate chip ice cream or other favorite frozen dessert

1. Combine raspberries, sugar, lemon juice, and mint extract in the workbowl of a large food processor. Process, scraping down sides several times, until sauce is smooth, about 30 seconds.

2. Pour sauce into a fine-mesh strainer set over a large bowl. Use a rubber spatula to press sauce through strainer and separate out the seeds. (It's fine if a few seeds make it into the sauce.)

3. Scoop ice cream into four bowls and drizzle each portion with several tablespoons of sauce. Serve immediately.

Tropical Sundae with Rum Toffee Sauce and Macadamia Nuts

Makes 4 sundaes
Time: 15 minutes

Can't afford a trip to the tropics? This sundae transports you to the islands in a matter of minutes. Although vanilla ice cream is suggested in the recipe, try a more exotic choice, like banana ice cream, for a true island flavor. Extra sauce can be refrigerated for several days and reheated in a microwave.

> ¼ cup chopped lightly salted macadamia nuts
> 1 cup firmly packed light brown sugar
> ⅓ cup heavy cream
> 8 tablespoons (1 stick) unsalted butter
> 1 tablespoon rum
> ½ teaspoon vanilla extract
> 1½ pints vanilla ice cream or other favorite
>   frozen dessert

1. Preheat oven to 350°. Spread nuts over a small baking sheet and toast until golden, about 5 minutes. Do not let nuts burn. Set aside.

2. Mix brown sugar, cream, butter, and rum in a small saucepan. Bring to a boil and simmer until sugar dissolves and sauce thickens a bit, about 2 minutes. Remove pan from heat and stir in vanilla extract. Cool sauce briefly.

3. Scoop ice cream into four bowls and drizzle each portion with several tablespoons of sauce. Sprinkle each sundae with 1 tablespoon toasted nuts. Serve immediately.

Vanilla Ice Cream Sundae with Peanut Butter Hot Fudge Sauce

Makes 4 sundaes
Time: 10 minutes

I prefer to use the more mellow European-style cocoa--also called Dutch-process cocoa--in this quick sundae recipe, although American-style cocoa works fine. Leftover sauce can be refrigerated for several days. Simply reheat in the micro wave and stir until smooth.

⅓ cup unsweetened cocoa

½ cup sugar

½ cup heavy cream

2 tablespoons creamy peanut butter

½ teaspoon vanilla extract

1½ pints vanilla ice cream or other favorite frozen dessert

Whipped cream, optional

Chopped nuts, such as peanuts, walnuts, or pecans, optional

1. Briefly whisk cocoa and sugar together in a small saucepan to remove any lumps. Slowly whisk in cream until smooth.
2. Set pan over medium heat. Bring sauce to the barest simmer, stirring occasionally to dissolve sugar. At the first sign of a boil, remove pan from heat and whisk in peanut butter and vanilla extract. Stir until smooth.
3. Scoop ice cream into four bowls and drizzle each portion with several tablespoons of sauce. Add whipped cream and chopped nuts, if desired. Serve immediately.

Creamy Rice Pudding with Raisins

Serves 4
Time: 45 minutes
(including 15 minutes for cooling)

This homey pudding is perfect on a cold winter's night. For extra richness, garnish the pudding with a dollop of whipped cream.

> 3½ cups milk
> ⅓ cup long-grain rice
> ⅓ cup raisins
> ¼ cup sugar
> 1 teaspoon vanilla extract
> Ground cinnamon, optional
> Whipped cream, optional

1. Combine milk, rice, raisins, and sugar in a medium saucepan. Bring mixture to a boil, stirring occasionally. Reduce heat to medium and partially cover.

2. Simmer pudding gently, stirring often, until most of the milk has been absorbed, 25 to 30 minutes. Remove pan from heat and stir in the vanilla extract.

3. Pour rice pudding into four custard cups or small bowls. Sprinkle with cinnamon, if desired. Cool slightly and serve warm with whipped cream, if desired.

Lemon Tapioca

Serves 4
Time: 40 minutes
(including 20 minutes for cooling)

1 cup – 8oz.
3/4   – 6
       – 4
       – 2

Warm tapioca pudding is the ultimate comfort food. In this version, lemon zest adds a spark while a beaten egg white makes the pudding lighter and fluffier.

1 large egg, separated
2 cups milk
3 tablespoons quick-cooking tapioca
¼ cup sugar plus 1 tablespoon
½ teaspoon finely grated lemon zest

1. Separate the egg. In a medium saucepan, combine the egg yolk, milk, tapioca, and ¼ cup sugar. Let stand for 5 minutes to swell tapioca.

2. Meanwhile, beat egg white with an electric mixer until frothy, about 30 seconds. Slowly add remaining tablespoon sugar and continue beating until whites form soft peaks. Beat in lemon zest and set aside.

3. Place saucepan with tapioca over medium heat and bring mixture to a boil, stirring occasionally. Gently simmer pudding for 1 minute then remove pan from heat.

4. Fold egg white mixture into hot pudding and pour tapioca into four custard cups or small bowls. Cool pudding until thickened, about 20 minutes. Serve warm.

Maple Bread Pudding

Serves 4
Time: 55 minutes
(including 15 minutes for cooling)

Recycle stale white bread in this warm dessert bursting with maple flavor. If only fresh bread is on hand, dry it out in a preheated 250° oven for 5 minutes. (Stale bread absorbs more liquid than fresh.) You will need between four to six slices of bread.

> 2 cups stale white bread cubes, cut into ½-inch pieces
>   (4 to 6 slices)
> 2 cups milk
> 2 tablespoons unsalted butter
> 2 large eggs plus 2 large egg yolks
> ½ cup maple syrup
> 1 teaspoon vanilla extract
> ½ teaspoon salt
> Confectioners' sugar for dusting, optional

1. Preheat oven to 350°. Butter four 1-cup ramekins or custard cups. Divide bread cubes evenly among the buttered cups.

2. Place milk and butter in a small saucepan set over medium heat. Stir occasionally until butter has melted and milk is hot but not boiling.

3. Separate 2 of the eggs, discarding whites or reserving for another use. Whisk the 2 eggs and 2 yolks with the maple syrup, vanilla extract, and salt in a large bowl. Slowly whisk in hot milk mixture. Immediately pour custard over bread cubes.

4. Bake puddings until tops are puffed and golden brown, about 30 minutes. Remove ramekins from oven and cool puddings on a rack. (Expect them to fall somewhat as they cool.) Dust puddings with confectioners' sugar, if desired, and serve warm.

Any Berry Crepes with Lemon Butter Sauce

Serves 4
Time: 30 minutes

Although this recipe looks complicated, the three components can be assembled in a matter of minutes. Fill the crepes with raspberries, blueberries, blackberries, or strawberries. If using strawberries, hull and thinly slice; leave smaller berries whole.

Berry Filling
1 generous pint fresh berries
1 tablespoon sugar

Vanilla Crepes
¾ cup milk
1 large egg
2 tablespoons vegetable oil
1 teaspoon vanilla extract
½ cup flour
1 tablespoon sugar
Pinch of salt
Vegetable oil spray, for cooking

L e m o n   B u t t e r   S a u c e
3 tablespoons butter
1 tablespoon lemon juice
2 teaspoons sugar
Confectioners' sugar for dusting filled crepes, optional

1. Place an ovenproof plate in the oven and preheat to 200°. Set a small skillet, measuring 7 or 8 inches, over medium-high heat.
2. For the filling, mix berries (see headnote about preparation, if necessary) and sugar in a medium bowl. Set aside to macerate fruit.
3. For crepes, place milk, egg, oil, and vanilla extract in the work bowl of a food processor. Process briefly until smooth. Add dry ingredients and process until smooth, scraping down sides of bowl once.
4. Place sauce ingredients in small pan and heat over low. Stir occasionally until butter and sugar have melted. Keep sauce warm.
5. Coat hot skillet with vegetable oil spray. Pour 3 tablespoons crepe batter into pan and tilt by the handle to swirl batter over the bottom of pan. Cook crepe until tiny bubbles cover top and edges are golden, about 1 minute. Use a thin metal spatula to lift edges of crepe and flip. Cook for another 30 seconds. Transfer crepe to plate in oven and repeat, greasing pan as needed, to make a total of 8 crepes.
6. Working with one crepe at a time, place best looking side of crepe face down. Line center of each crepe with some of the fruit. Roll crepes and place two on each plate. Drizzle with sauce and dust lightly with confectioners' sugar, if desired.

Apple Raspberry Crisp

Serves 6
Time: 50 minutes

This is one of my all-time favorite desserts. It's delicious and remarkably easy to make. I bake this nut-topped crisp every week during the early fall when both local raspberries and apples are in season near my home.

4 medium tart apples such as McIntosh
1 pint fresh raspberries
½ cup chopped walnuts
¾ cup flour
⅓ cup firmly packed brown sugar
1 tablespoon granulated sugar
⅛ teaspoon ground cinnamon
⅛ teaspoon salt
5 tablespoons unsalted butter
Vanilla ice cream or whipped cream, optional

1. Preheat oven to 375°. Peel, core, and thinly slice apples. Arrange apples in an 8- or 9-inch-square ovenproof ceramic or glass pan that measures about 2 inches deep. Spread raspberries over apples. The fruit should come three-quarters of the way up the sides of the pan.

2. Make topping by combining nuts, flour, brown sugar, granulated sugar, cinnamon, and salt in a small bowl. Cut butter into ½-inch pieces and toss into bowl. Cut butter into nut mixture with fingers or a fork.

3. Sprinkle topping evenly over fruit in pan. Bake until fruit is bubbling and topping turns golden brown, about 35 minutes. Serve warm with vanilla ice cream or whipped cream, if desired.

Baked Apples with Raisins and Walnuts

Makes 4 apples
Time: 55 minutes

Choose large, firm baking apples such as Macouns, Romes, or Winesaps for this dish. Fill the cored apples with raisins and brown sugar, brush them with butter, then roll in ground walnuts that have been scented with cinnamon.

4 tablespoons unsalted butter
½ cup walnuts
¼ cup granulated sugar
½ teaspoon cinnamon
⅓ cup raisins
¼ cup firmly packed brown sugar
4 large baking apples (about 2 pounds)
½ cup apple juice or cider
Heavy cream or vanilla ice cream, optional

1. Preheat oven to 400°. Melt butter and set aside.
2. Place nuts, granulated sugar, and cinnamon in the work

bowl of a food processor and grind until nuts are quite fine. Set mixture aside in a shallow bowl.

4. Combine raisins and brown sugar in another bowl.

5. Core the apples, then carefully remove the top half of the peel from each. Fill hollow centers with the raisin-brown sugar mixture. Brush peeled portions of apples with butter, then roll in walnut mixture until bare sections are well coated. Place apples in a small baking dish. Drizzle with remaining butter. Pour apple juice into bottom of pan.

6. Bake until crust on apples turns golden brown and centers can be easily pierced with a knife, 35 to 40 minutes. Serve warm with juices from pan and heavy cream or vanilla ice cream, if desired.

Baked Banana Splits with Orange Butterscotch Sauce

Makes 4 sundaes
Time: 25 minutes

Roasting bananas in their skins brings out the full flavor of the fruit. The orange-flavored butterscotch sauce complements their tropical overtones and a scoop of vanilla ice cream adds creamy richness.

4 ripe but not mushy bananas, unpeeled
⅓ cup orange juice
½ cup firmly packed light brown sugar
3 tablespoons unsalted butter
1 pint vanilla ice cream or other favorite frozen dessert

1. Preheat oven to 350°. Place whole bananas on a baking sheet and roast until skins blacken, about 10 minutes. Remove

bananas from oven and cool until skins are only warm to the touch, 5 to 10 minutes.

2. While bananas are in the oven, place orange juice, brown sugar, and butter in a small saucepan set over medium heat. Bring to a boil and simmer gently for several minutes to dissolve sugar. Remove sauce from heat and cool slightly. (Sauce will be fairly thin.)

3. Use a small sharp knife to slit cooled banana skins. Peel and discard skins. Slice bananas in half lengthwise.

4. Place a split banana in each of four dessert bowls. Top each banana with a large scoop of vanilla ice cream and drizzle with some of the butterscotch sauce. Serve immediately.

Baked Peaches with Amaretti Cookies

Serves 4
Time: 20 minutes

Amaretti are almond-flavored Italian macaroons. These not-too-sweet cookies are wonderful with any fruit, especially peaches and nectarines, either of which can be used in this recipe. Look for amaretti at Italian markets and gourmet stores. This dessert can be embellished with heavy cream (either whipped or straight from the refrigerator) or vanilla ice cream.

> **2 tablespoons unsalted butter**
> **2 tablespoons sugar**
> **8 medium amaretti cookies**
> **4 ripe but not mushy peaches**
> **Heavy cream or vanilla ice cream, optional**

1. Preheat oven to 400°. Coat a ceramic baking or gratin dish with ½ tablespoon butter. Cut remaining butter into 8 pieces and reserve. Sprinkle dish with 1 tablespoon of the sugar.
2. Place cookies in a plastic bag and seal. Crush lightly with a mallet. There should be about ½ cup amaretti crumbs.
3. Use a small, sharp knife to slice peaches in half, making sure to cut through the stem end to facilitate removal of the pit. Remove pits and place peach halves, cut side up, into the prepared dish.
4. Place one piece of reserved butter into each peach half. Sprinkle peaches with remaining tablespoon sugar. Sprinkle cookie crumbs over fruit.
5. Place dish in center of oven and bake for 10 minutes. Turn oven to broil and place dish several inches from heat source. Broil until tops are bubbly and light brown, about 2 minutes. Do not let cookie crumbs burn. Serve peaches immediately with heavy cream or vanilla ice cream, if desired.

Best-Ever Blueberry Cobbler

Serves 6
Time: 55 minutes

This summery dessert is easy to prepare. Toss blueberries with a bit of sugar and orange juice, then cover with a simple sugar cookie dough. The crust becomes crisp and golden in the oven, while the berries form a thick filling. Frozen blueberries can be used during the off season.

3 cups blueberries
½ cup sugar plus 3 tablespoons
⅓ cup orange juice
⅔ cup flour
¼ teaspoon baking powder
Pinch of salt
8 tablespoons (1 stick) unsalted butter, softened
1 large egg
½ teaspoon vanilla extract
Whipped cream or vanilla ice cream, optional

1. Preheat oven to 375°. Toss berries, 3 tablespoons sugar, and orange juice in an 8-inch-square ovenproof glass or ceramic dish that measures about 2 inches deep. Set dish aside.

2. Whisk flour, baking powder, and salt together in a small bowl. Set aside.

3. Cream butter and remaining ½ cup sugar in an electric mixer until fluffy and light in color. Beat in egg and vanilla extract until smooth. Slowly incorporate dry ingredients using low setting on mixer.

4. Drop batter by rounded tablespoons over berry filling. Cover as much of the surface as possible with small clumps of batter. Some uncovered spots will remain but drop batter so that the open areas are as small as possible.

5. Bake cobbler until crust is golden brown and berry filling is bubbling, 35 to 40 minutes. Remove pan from oven and cool briefly. Serve as is or with whipped cream or vanilla ice cream.

Caramelized Pineapple Slices with Toasted Pecans

Serves 4
Time: 10 minutes

This recipe is remarkably quick and quite delicious. As long as you own a pineapple corer, this dessert can also be made with fresh pineapple. (This handy device removes the core in one piece and makes it possible to cut a peeled pineapple into rings.) Serve the pineapple rings as is or over vanilla ice cream or frozen yogurt for a hot-and-cold tropical dessert.

> 1 can (20 ounces) pineapple slices packed
>   in unsweetened juice
> ¼ cup firmly packed light brown sugar
> ⅓ cup finely chopped pecans or macadamia nuts
> Vanilla ice cream or frozen yogurt, optional

1. Place oven rack several inches below broiler and preheat broiler.

2. Line a small baking sheet with aluminum foil. Drain pineapple and place slices on the foil-lined baking sheet. Sprinkle sugar and then nuts over the pineapple.

3. Broil pineapple until sugar is bubbling and nuts are toasted, 2 to 4 minutes. (Timing depends on distance between baking sheet and heat source.)

4. Remove baking sheet from oven and use a spatula to transfer pineapple slices to plates. Serve immediately with vanilla ice cream or frozen yogurt, if desired.

Plum Shortcakes

Makes 4 shortcakes
Time: 35 minutes

Buttery biscuits can be paired with any fresh fruit. Although this version calls for plums, an equal amount of peaches or nectarines or one pint of strawberries or blueberries can be used instead.

Biscuits
1 cup flour
1½ teaspoons baking powder
¼ teaspoon salt
2 teaspoons sugar
4 tablespoons unsalted butter
⅓ cup milk

Plum Filling
4 ripe plums (about ¾ pound)
2 tablespoons sugar

Whipped Cream
½ cup chilled heavy cream
1 tablespoon confectioners' sugar

1. Preheat oven to 425°. Grease a small baking sheet.

2. For the biscuits, place flour, baking powder, salt, and 1½ teaspoons of the sugar in the work bowl of a food processor and pulse briefly to mix ingredients. Cut butter into 4 pieces and add to work bowl. Process until mixture resembles coarse crumbs, about 20 seconds. With motor running, add milk and process until dough forms a rough ball.

3. Drop dough into 4 mounds on the prepared baking sheet. Leave at least 2 inches between roughly shaped biscuits. Sprinkle tops with remaining ½ teaspoon sugar.

4. Bake biscuits until tops are golden brown, about 15 minutes. Transfer to a rack and cool for 10 minutes.

5. While biscuits are baking, half plums and remove the pits. Cut halves into thin slices. Toss plum slices with sugar in a bowl. Set fruit aside, stirring occasionally, until sugar has dissolved and a thin syrup has formed, about 20 minutes.

6. Beat heavy cream with confectioners' sugar just until it holds soft peaks. Keep refrigerated until serving time.

7. Use a serrated knife to carefully slice tops from cooled biscuits. Place each bottom half in a dessert bowl. Spoon some of the fruit and the syrup over the biscuit. Top with a generous dollop of whipped cream and then cover with more fruit. Place top of biscuit over fruit and cream and serve immediately.

Passions

Belgian Chocolate Waffles With Ice Cream

Serves 4
Time: 20 minutes

Spike thick Belgian waffles with chocolate and then top them with a scoop of ice cream--chocolate or vanilla are my two top choices--for a fast treat. Make sure to grease the waffle iron well before use. Note that the recipe makes two cups of batter, enough for four 5-inch square waffles. If your iron makes larger waffles, the yield will be lower.

4 tablespoons unsalted butter
2 ounces unsweetened chocolate
½ cup flour
½ teaspoon baking powder
¼ teaspoon salt
½ cup sugar
2 large eggs
1 teaspoon vanilla extract
2 tablespoons milk
1 pint chocolate or vanilla ice cream

1. Melt butter and chocolate together in the top of a double boiler or in a microwave, stirring occasionally until smooth. Set aside to cool slightly.

2. Whisk flour, baking powder, and salt together in a small bowl. Set aside.

3. Combine sugar, eggs, and vanilla extract in a large bowl. Stir in cooled chocolate mixture. Fold in dry ingredients, alternating with a tablespoon of milk at a time, until batter is smooth. Do not overbeat.

4. Heat waffle iron and lightly grease the grids with vegetable oil spray. Pour ½ cup batter over grids. (Use more for large grids.) Close waffle iron and cook until waffle is well done, 3 to 4 minutes.

5. Remove waffle from iron and top with a scoop of ice cream. Repeat process with remaining batter. (If desired, baked waffles can be kept warm in a 200° oven before being topped with ice cream.)

Chocolate Chocolate Chip Cookies

Makes 24 cookies
Time: 30 minutes

These extra-chocolatey cookies are an easy variation on the familiar Tollhouse recipe. They are loaded with chocolate chips and nuts.

1 cup flour
¼ cup unsweetened cocoa
½ teaspoon baking soda
½ teaspoon salt
8 tablespoons (1 stick) unsalted butter, softened
¾ cup sugar
1 large egg
½ teaspoon vanilla extract
1 cup (6 ounces) chocolate chips
½ cup chopped walnuts

1. Preheat oven to 375°.
2. Briefly whisk flour, cocoa, baking soda, and salt together in a small bowl. Set aside.

3. Use an electric mixer to cream butter and sugar until fluffy and light in color. Beat in egg and vanilla until smooth. Slowly beat in the dry ingredients. Stir in the chocolate chips and nuts.

4. Drop heaping tablespoons of batter at least one inch apart onto two ungreased baking sheets. Bake until edges and tops of cookies are set, about 12 minutes. Transfer cookies to a rack and cool briefly.

Double Mocha Brownies

**Makes 12 small brownies
Time: 60 minutes
(including 20 minutes for cooling)**

Kahlua adds a smooth coffee flavor to these fudgy brownies, while instant coffee granules deliver a strong java jolt. Do not overbake brownies; remove them from the oven after 25 minutes, even if a toothpick comes out moist.

8 tablespoons (1 stick) unsalted butter
2 ounces unsweetened chocolate
1 tablespoon Kahlua or other coffee liqueur
1 teaspoon instant coffee granules
⅔ cup flour
½ teaspoon baking powder
¼ teaspoon salt
1 cup sugar
2 large eggs
1 teaspoon vanilla extract

1. Preheat oven to 350°. Grease an 8-inch-square baking pan.
2. Place butter, chocolate, Kahlua, and instant coffee in a small saucepan set over low heat. Stir occasionally until butter and

chocolate have melted. (Or, microwave ingredients on medium power until melted, about 1½ minutes. Stir until smooth.) Set mixture aside to cool briefly.

3. Whisk flour, baking powder, and salt together in a small bowl. Set aside.

4. Stir sugar into slightly cooled chocolate mixture. Beat in eggs and vanilla until smooth. Fold in dry ingredients and scrape batter into prepared pan.

5. Bake until toothpick inserted halfway between edge and center of pan comes out clean, 22 to 25 minutes. Do not over-bake. Transfer pan to a rack and cut brownies when cool.

Easiest-Ever Chocolate Souffles

Makes 4 souffles
Time: 50 minutes

*This cross between a baked pudding and a souffle is incredibly rich.
Room temperature eggs are able to hold more air than cold eggs
when beaten. Refrigerated eggs can be quickly warmed in water, as
directed in the recipe. Baking part of the souffles in a water bath
tames the heat of the oven and ensures a moist texture.*

> 6 ounces semisweet or bittersweet chocolate
> 8 tablespoons (1 stick) unsalted butter
> 4 large eggs
> 1 cup flour
> ½ teaspoon baking powder
> ¼ teaspoon salt
> 1 teaspoon vanilla extract
> 1 cup sugar
> Confectioners' sugar for dusting souffles

1. Preheat oven to 350°. Place a large baking pan in
the center of the oven and fill with about ½ inch of
warm water.
2. Melt chocolate and butter together in the top of a double

boiler or a microwave, stirring occasionally until smooth. Set aside to cool slightly.

3. While chocolate and butter are melting, place uncracked eggs in a small bowl and cover with warm water. Set aside for 5 minutes.

4. Whisk flour, baking powder, and salt together in a small bowl. Set aside.

5. Crack eggs into a large bowl and add vanilla extract. Beat with an electric mixer until foamy, about 1 minute. Add sugar and beat on medium-high until mixture thickens and lightens in color, about 2 minutes. Stir in cooled chocolate mixture, then gently fold in dry ingredients.

6. Pour batter into four 1-cup ramekins or custard cups. (Batter will come almost to the rims.) Carefully place filled ramekins in baking pan, making sure that water comes no higher than one-third of the way up the sides of the cups.

7. Bake until tops of souffles are firm to the touch and slightly cracked, about 30 minutes. Gently remove ramekins from water and cool for 5 minutes. Dust lightly with confectioners' sugar and serve warm.

Midnight Chocolate Pudding

Serves 4
Time: 30 minutes
(including 10 minutes for cooling)

Cocoa provides the punch, semisweet chocolate the smoothness in this decadent, dark pudding. Extra servings can be wrapped in plastic and refrigerated overnight.

½ cup sugar

⅓ cup unsweetened cocoa

2 tablespoons cornstarch

2 cups milk

2 ounces semisweet or bittersweet chocolate

2 tablespoons unsalted butter

1 teaspoon vanilla extract

1. Whisk sugar, cocoa, and cornstarch in a medium saucepan to break up any lumps. Slowly whisk in milk and set pan over medium heat.

2. Heat mixture, stirring often, especially as mixture thickens and comes to a boil. Let pudding simmer gently for 1 minute, stirring constantly to prevent scorching.

3. Stir in chocolate and butter. As soon as they have melted, remove pan from heat and stir in vanilla.

4. Pour pudding into four custard cups or small bowls. Cool slightly and serve warm.

Applesauce Date Bars

Makes 12 bars
Time: 40 minutes
(including 10 minutes for cooling)

These cake-like bars get their moist, chewy texture from applesauce, which replaces much of the fat that is otherwise required in baked goods. Raisins can be substituted for the dates, if desired.

> 2 tablespoons canola or vegetable oil
> ½ cup applesauce
> ⅔ cup firmly packed brown sugar
> 1 teaspoon vanilla extract
> 1 large egg
> 1 cup flour
> ¼ teaspoon baking soda
> ½ teaspoon ground cinnamon
> ¼ teaspoon ground allspice
> ½ cup chopped dates

1. Preheat oven to 350°. Grease an 8-inch-square baking pan.
2. Combine oil, applesauce, brown sugar, and vanilla extract with an electric mixer. Beat in egg until smooth.
3. Whisk flour, baking soda, cinnamon, and allspice together in a small bowl. Stir dry ingredients into batter and mix until just combined. Stir in dates.
4. Pour batter into prepared pan. Bake until edges begin to pull away from the sides of the pan and a toothpick inserted in the center of pan comes out clean, 20 to 25 minutes. Cool pan on a rack and cut into bars.

Guilt-free Cocoa Brownies

Makes 12 bars
Time: 45 minutes
(including 15 minutes for cooling)

Brownie lovers can throw caution to the wind when enjoying these moist, rich bars that have just one-third the fat found in traditional recipes. The secret is unsweetened cocoa, which has three grams of fat per ounce as compared to 15 grams per ounce in baking chocolate. Nonfat sour cream and extra egg whites help keep the brownies moist without adding fat.

½ cup flour
½ cup unsweetened cocoa
½ teaspoon baking powder
¼ teaspoon salt
1 large egg plus 2 large egg whites
4 tablespoons unsalted butter
¼ cup nonfat sour cream
2 teaspoons vanilla extract
1 cup sugar

1. Preheat oven to 350°. Grease an 8-inch-square baking pan.
2. Whisk flour, cocoa, baking powder, and salt together in a medium bowl. Set aside. Separate the 2 egg whites, discarding the yolks or reserving for another use. Set aside with whole egg.
3. Melt butter and cool slightly. Whisk sour cream and vanilla into butter. Beat in sugar, and then the egg and egg whites. Fold in cocoa mixture and mix until well combined.
4. Pour batter into prepared pan and bake until toothpick inserted halfway between center and edge of pan comes out fairly clean, about 22 minutes. (A few fudgy crumbs should cling to the toothpick but not liquidy batter.) Cool pan on a rack and cut brownies when cool.

Honeydew Melon in Sweet Basil Syrup

Serves 4
Time: 30 minutes

An aromatic syrup flavored with basil, cloves, white wine, and orange juice lends a gentle sweetness to pieces of honeydew melon. Cantaloupe or other flavorful melon can be used in this recipe. Refrigerate leftover melon in the syrup for several days.

> ½ cup white wine
> ½ cup sugar
> ¼ cup chopped fresh basil leaves, plus 4 sprigs
>   for garnish, optional
> 4 whole cloves
> ¼ cup orange juice
> Ice cubes
> 1 honeydew melon (about 3½ to 4 pounds)

1. Combine wine, sugar, basil, and cloves in a small saucepan. Bring mixture to a boil, stirring occasionally to dissolve sugar. Simmer for 3 minutes.

2. While syrup is heating, pour orange juice into a heatproof glass measuring cup. Add enough ice cubes to raise liquid to ⅔ cup line.

3. Pour hot sugar syrup through a fine-mesh strainer and directly into the measuring cup. Discard solids.

4. While syrup cools to room temperature, remove seeds and rind from melon and cut into 1-inch chunks. Place melon pieces in a glass or ceramic bowl and cover with cooled syrup. Let stand for at least 15 minutes to infuse melon with flavor.

5. Divide melon pieces among four bowls, adding several tablespoons of syrup to each portion. (Some of the syrup will remain unused.) Serve immediately with a sprig of fresh basil, if desired.

Macerated Strawberries with Balsamic Vinegar

Serves 4

Time: 35 minutes

When fresh berries are tossed with sugar and left to stand, the sugar slowly dissolves and forms a rich syrup. Best of all, even not-so-sweet berries burst with flavor. A touch of balsamic vinegar balances the sweetness and gives the syrup even more body.

> 2 pints fresh strawberries
> 3 to 4 tablespoons sugar
> 1 tablespoon balsamic vinegar

1. Hull berries and trim any unripe portions. Slice small berries in half; cut larger berries into three or four thick slices. In either case, cut from the stem end through the pointed bottom of the berries.

2. Place sliced berries in a large glass or ceramic bowl and

toss gently with 3 tablespoons sugar. If berries are particularly tart, add 1 more tablespoon sugar.

3. Let berries macerate at room temperature, tossing occasionally, to help the sugar to dissolve. After about 30 minutes, the sugar will have formed a thick, red syrup.

4. Gently toss macerated berries with vinegar. Divide berries and syrup among four bowls or glass goblets. Serve immediately.

Pears and Parmesan Drizzled with Honey

Serves 4
Time: 10 minutes

This easy but elegant snack will satisfy the sophisticated nosher who wants a hint of sweetness but no more. The finest Parmesan, preferable Parmigiano-Reggiano, should be used.

2 large ripe pears
Small hunk of Parmesan cheese (at least 2 ounces)
4 teaspoons honey

1. Core and thinly slice the pears. Arrange slices on four dessert plates.
2. Use a vegetable peeler to remove long, paper-thin curls from the piece of Parmesan. Place a cheese curl between each slice of pear on the plates.
3. Measure honey into a small bowl and microwave briefly (no more than 20 seconds) to make it easier to pour. Use a small spoon to drizzle honey slowly over the four plates. Serve at once.

Vanilla Frozen Yogurt with Strawberry Ginger Sauce

Serves 4
Time: 10 minutes

Ground ginger brightens a warm strawberry sauce that is the perfect foil to vanilla frozen yogurt. If you use nonfat yogurt, this sundae is fat-free. Try making a similar sauce with blueberries and cinnamon.

> 1 pint fresh strawberries
> 2 tablespoons sugar
> 2 tablespoons water
> ½ teaspoon ground ginger
> 1½ pints vanilla frozen yogurt

1. Hull and slice strawberries into several pieces. Toss berries with sugar, water, and ginger in a small saucepan.
2. Set saucepan over medium heat and bring liquid to a boil. Lightly mash some of the berries with a fork and continue

simmering until the juices thicken a bit, about 1 minute.
Remove pan from heat and let sauce cool for several minutes.
3. Scoop frozen yogurt into four bowls. Spoon several tablespoons of the warm strawberry sauce over each portion and
serve immediately.

LIQUID AND DRY MEASURE EQUIVALENCIES

Customary	Metric
¼ teaspoon	1.25 milliliters
½ teaspoon	2.5 milliliters
1 teaspoon	5 milliliters
1 tablespoon	15 milliliters
1 fluid ounce	30 milliliters
¼ cup	60 milliliters
⅓ cup	80 milliliters
½ cup	120 milliliters
1 cup	240 milliliters
1 pint (2 cups)	680 milliliters
1 quart (4 cups; 32 ounces)	960 milliliters (.96 liter)
1 gallon (4 quarts)	3.84 liters
1 ounce (by weight)	28 grams
¼ pound (4 ounces)	114 grams
1 pound (16 ounces)	454 grams
2.2 pounds	1 kilogram (1,000 grams)

OVEN TEMPERATURE EQUIVALENTS

Description	°Fahrenheit	°Celsius
Cool	200	90
Very slow	250	120
Slow	300–325	150–160
Moderately slow	325–350	160–180
Moderate	350–375	180–190
Moderately hot	375–400	190–200
Hot	400–450	200–230
Very hot	450–500	230–260